The Experiment of the Tropics

The Experiment of the Tropics

POEMS

Lawrence
Lacambra Ypil

Published by Gaudy Boy LLC,
an imprint of Singapore Unbound
www.singaporeunbound.org/gaudyboy
New York

For more information on ordering books, contact jkoh@singaporeunbound.org.

ISBN 978-0-9828142-5-3

Cover design by Flora Chan
Interior design by Christina Newhard
Proofread by Cindy Hochman of "100 Proof" Copyediting Services

Table of Contents

The Experiment of the Tropics

There Is a River

There is a river. And then there is a man.

There is a skirt. And then there is a woman, three women, their feet dipped
in the water.

A dam is built in Bolocboloc and it is called progress.

A dam is built in Bolocboloc and families on weekends congregate in circles to
watch the show of water spilling from the mouth of a river to the mouth of a
wall.

It is magic, says the girl standing at the edge of the pool tilting her head to the
right. *It is magic,*

says the man holding his arms above the water waving his arms
above a stream that has been conjured first out of a bush then out of a
cliff then out of a pipe that runs through miles across a city, miles across
through towns where the corn is planted and the harvest reaped where the fish
is snared into a net and then hauled into a ship where a church is built, coral
by coral, until it is deemed a fitting place to worship. *TA-DA!*

Magic happens by a trick of light and a gesture repeated, says the man
who stands at the cusp of where a jet of water falls into a pool
and creates out of his hands a spectacle out of an altogether natural thing.

A woman holds up a cup made of coconut husk into the air.

A daughter smiles, her foot in the water on a stone, because she has been
told all her life that she is beautiful and she believes it.

The Nature of a City

The nature of a city depends on the direction its people are moving. In the morning, *towards*. By evening, *away*. The wealth of a city depends on the density of this movement and its speed. There is conflicting evidence to suggest that the slow pace of traffic moving away from the center of the city at six in the afternoon, past the pharmacy at the corner into the wide industrial roads that cut through the fields of fallow over six small bridges and six thin rivers into the smaller and smaller towns until one gets to a house with the light left on in the kitchen is the best indicator of a city's development or demise. It takes bringing something into the heart of a city, then back out into its tributaries, to raise the price of one's possessions. This principle applies to one's hopes and desires as it does to chickens and vegetables. There is hardly any evidence left, but years ago a train cut through the center of the island northeast to southwest, parallel to the shore. Or southwest *to* northeast depending on whether one was coming home for dinner, or one was going against the current, meaning going back to the city because one had left the key to a cabinet that one had been planning to open for a very long time.

There Is a Chair but No One Sits

There is a chair but no one sits. There is a flag but there is no wind.

      Stars and stripes. Sun and sand make good weather.

There is a cabana on a ship. A slip. A skirt

      is what a woman holds of another and asks, "Where at?"

"How much?"   Style as a way of asking without asking

      for a name: sigh: below: the temporary address of a blank

look   or a quick comeback made in retrospect

      or the double-take of *then*   *now*   *never*   or the return of the sideburn—

A stranger checked her out but already her arm was hooked under a brother's.

A party was a crowd gathered into the smallest area possible,

      where everyone looked at anywhere else except at the camera.

That collection made on the faintest trace of *there, there, dear sir,*

       if you can walk towards the gangplank

       if you can walk towards the gangplank and be still.

How Does Love Begin

How does love begin? By song and dance.   By chance.

There is a song and a woman steps up to the podium.

For every song of loss, there is a song of redemption. For every woman,

       a man who stands behind her looking at his fingers

        while he strums a guitar, knowing his music is background to her voice

       so he keeps it on the low side.

Longing is a head turned away towards a century.

Singing needs a somewhere else across an ocean, beyond a mountain.

Meanwhile, a lark sitting on a bough sings over and over till we sleep.

Meanwhile, a woman and a man step onstage: the woman to sing, the man on his

       strings, even if this time around they do it not for love or devotion but for

       stereo.

For the first time in the city, the stage that is here becomes elsewhere.

       By airwave and speaker.

               Now we are all in this together:

        on our feet   in our sleep   a wind enters

     and does not leave—

The first time I received a letter from a boy, he asked:

       "When can I kiss you?"

Now we will never be alone: A man will pause for effect.

     A woman will breathe   before the high note.

          Almost simultaneous.

A Game Occurs

A game occurs the moment concentric circles form around a core. In a field of grass, for example, watch how a group of boys gathers around the sudden spectacle of a foot pressed firmly against a ball. Watch the boys look first at the ball, and then at each other. Who'll kick the ball? Where is the goal? Who is the captain of the team? The goal and the captain are optional. Meanwhile, the ball shifts direction as it hits a knee and then crosses a fence's boundary. Now it is in danger of slipping down a slope of stones into a river or flying over the branches of a neighbor's tree or getting stuck on a roof. The game ends when the goal becomes a broken window or the sea.

A Hat Tipped

What is more tempting than a hat tipped precariously on a knee?

Not me.

What is more touching than a hand laid gently at the edge of the sea?

An arm placed over the shoulder of a stranger is surely just a sign of camaraderie.

Certainly.

The Experiment of the Tropics

As a nest among the trees   As a garden among the bigger garden of the sea

      Mountain   View   As a wish that were drawn to scale

So the idea became foldable   a mere scaffold

      Discarded   For that long-lasting thing

That revivalist thing   style   which as the master

      carpenter implied   went beyond   Road   Port

Nut   Bolt   Wharf   A nail

      In a railroad   A pipe

          that opened and closed

      The central portico   The color and the texture of

      a solid colonnade   of *Inday's* silence

      which was her sense of water flowing   across the experiment

that was the tropics: A riverbank made private

      A theater of night guards   A soda parlor

      Of that foreign good   whiskey tractor

red tin can   with the picture of a scarab   and a quaker oat

      Acquisition   That American thing

      The good old good

      Cheese and grape

There was a tennis court in the club   where you hit a ball

      and nothing returned.

      We munched   on its brandy biscuit.

      We ordered two of it.

No Minstrel without a Hat

No minstrel without a hat.

   No shoe without a leg crossed.

  A hand was where a man   could lean his cheek

against a window ledge   and look over a field

  while another clutched his throat   *Casa*

  being a promontory   for somewhere else

  or out on the street   where the men sat

  with their guitars.

No face without an eye closed.   No shore

   Where the hand parted the hair

    Where the *karosa* passed on its way back to church

     And in that soft *ventanilla* splendor of

   Strum   Shudder   Yawn

There was a name written   but only for the sister sold

  On the idea of *where else?*   but under the eaves

Where the animals are kept   beside the carriages

   and *once, there was the music.*   Then nothing else.

The Extent to Which Someone Else's Labor

To the extent that someone else's labor could subsume itself

        into a patch of color

        so it became by default   a petal

          when looked at from afar:

             I put my feelings once into a photograph

             I pressed my foot twice on that pedal:

     Stitch to the eye   Finger

on that finger of history   to the extent that I could imagine repetition

        enough to make a dress.

        What made me think

that if I matched the shine of my boot   with a saber

       and untied the shoes   of that man on the other side

               of some *carpet lush*

   shimmer   shoulder   strap and buckle

on a chair chiseled by leisure, loss, so I could merely

position myself   in relation to who I could become

     so the wave of another sea

       could press on me differently.

Shrub and Bush

In the American style of learning by lying

on the lawn and that new Baroque interior of labor: craft

      that filigreed stitch of gold

      and shrub and bush   and heft and wood   that school of soil

      on the grounds of how to work   by talking about work:

      No lace.   No song.

Nothing was real unless it moved.

      No slouch.   No South.

No elsewhere was that transposable spite of weather.

That picture of a cliff without a stone.

Of grass to hold.

By forest tended.   By music melded

In the attempt to understand inertia or the notion that yours

      And mine and ours was measured by the distance

from the side of the road, which was otherwise called a porch.

No Gramophone's No Face

No gramophone's no face

      No pineapple's reversed

            In the way a man leans against the post   to signify

                Come   *Here*

while another looks

      In the hammock of brass pots, a tablecloth, a lamp, a woman taking the gloss of glass, a man holding a placard with the word *Revel* in reverse as a stand-in for a gold-embossed bone that was thrown with the figure lacquer to the grass.

We were willing islands, really.

We held hands, briefly,

      between stamen and trinket   cymbal and sand

      and there was a way to hold a saucer and its cover

      so it could be sold   as a hammer

to the brother on a ship, thinking

      he would still build a house of stilts by the river.

By the stream.

For Every Man

For every man that stumbles into a room
feeling for the door, asking himself, "What did I wish
to do here now that I've come?"
there is a man who stays inside.

He had a good eye once that one who squinted
against the light that slipped through a crack
the way a buckle would slip through a hole to keep
the neck from turning, the tongue from falling.

Spittle left on grit teeth when it swayed
among the leaves. Birds' wings flattened
the banana trees as in the war of every man
that chose not to speak to himself

but chose instead to draw his signature
across a face the way a body
disemboweled itself. No body
"disembowels itself." It takes two men.

In the Time It Takes

In the time it takes for the shadow of the world

    to reach the shadow of the knee

of the woman sitting in the park under a tree

        a photograph is developed.

Drip, drip, splash.

    Then alright.

      Then a dry mount

      against the *wet, wet* grass.

When the city's architects asked what could be done with the past,

they didn't anticipate glass.   They believed the ocean

with its endless shimmer of *always* would make the dame denizens

of the city sick from squinting at the sea.

What reprieve the streets could be, what rain

    falling endlessly from the eaves of shophouses

      as a line of trees becomes the token gesture

    nature makes to signify an elsewhere here

where a woman slowly rises to become the shadow of a shadow of me.

A Fashion Is a Fashion

The difficulty of the law   as it was written.

The difficulty of love   as demeanor: *If you let it so*

What: a novel   What: a figure in a suit

    The slack   pants are made of

      What landscape.

I moved a chair once   to face the window

    thinking this was what I needed: to fold one's legs

                to let one's hair go.

We took from the war what we wanted:

      a three-button jacket

      a uniform for home   which was a vest, really

        with some really long lapel

where the fold folded over

    where: *I could not hold what held*   a silhouette of hunger

    where: the cuff hurt

where the sleeve almost reached the wrist

and one's pants could not cover the shoe so you had

    to raise it. A leg.

A fist of nothing.   Just sitting there

    looking at the distance   a stray strand of hair

the strip of stripe   of here and there and here again

        and in that particular hierarchy of relation.

A Hankie in the Breast Pocket

A hankie in the breast pocket was for the sniffles.

A bowtie around the neck was for the rest.

In the way the lone bud extended forlornly

Towards the ear of the man in the picture

as if it were the hand of his lover reaching

from across the bed to part his hair—

If we asked him where he was, would he say *here?*

In the studio where there was a window

that opened to that mind of summer

where a vase's gold etching matched

the carpet matched the tip of the slick

after which he washed his face. Flush.

Flick. If only the tight lapel of that steel rose

pierced his heart—Oh grace of some yesteryear

romance of someone far he was thinking of

with his lips pursed. If only the wood etching

of the chair would leave a mark on his palm.

Where Is the Goddess

In the crook of a finger   In the chink of a cup

      In the outline of an arm seen briefly   by slant of light

         In the painting at least   she held the hand of her sister

            by the banister.

Somewhere else: "summer" and "fall"

Somewhere else: mud stuck on the soles of shoes

        you needed a branch   to pry it loose.

A bouffant was a way to hold her hair in place

     in the face of history.   A dress to lay a flower on

       so petal to petal   became both lover

         and not there   lying on the grass

   a skirt as foliage   and wind

   so hold your gaze   dear stranger

        pointing to no one in particular

               Here.

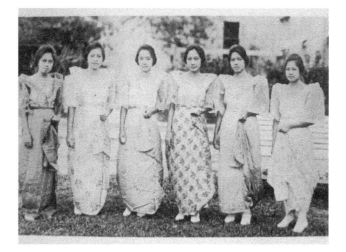

What Is the Erotic

Water from a rock, river from a jug, that foreign thing: the hour, which is what you
are: self seen through stealth, telescope.

To untie the knot. To let a ship sail into the ocean without coming back. To steam
the afternoon with merely your breath. Your father's barber cuts your hair and
holds your cheek against the blade, while you rub your elbow against his crotch.
When letting a stranger stick a needle into your ear without flinching, what makes
you trust a woman and not a man. What makes you have the nails of your foot so
clean they shine when you are sitting at the store-corner with only your slippers on.

A street is a way of watching a movie when you don't have money. Always moving,
ever moving poem about some Virginia, while a man in the corner checks out the
lady getting onto the jeepney on the way to work. That you see him touch himself
is what becomes you. That someone else's labor levitates you off your bed to the
breakfast table where, *voila,* the food is served, and later back in your room, *voila,*
you find your bedspread flattened, the shirt pressed, your socks folded on the bed's
edge, is what makes you sing in the morning.

Will you not sit, sir, and put on a pair of pants. and then the other. Will you not slip
your foot into one of them shiny shoes you would lick off of if only it were worn by
the driver your father pays to bring you to school.

What is erotic is how slick your hair is, how clean, how you stare off into space
when you are singing while he is speaking, how you appear to look at him, how you
appear to him, how you are wearing a pair of shades, how you are crossing your
legs. Old enough to be a father, young enough to be a son. A uniform is the far-off

look we make that is really the shadow made by money in order for you to be driven home. The invention of the machine that would allow the sound of breathing to be the most stimulating thing. To wait for directions. To read the script again. To begin somewhere midway. To pretend.

In the Manner of Thinking

In the manner of thinking

        that is the thinking of the boy

                sitting on a chair   with his legs crossed

      believing this is what thinking does

                    resting his elbow on his knee

        staring at the ground pretending

this is what looking does   to looking.

                         In the garden,

the photographer held the flower   by its stem

      while the maid   thinking this was what believing meant

        looked into the distance of herself   while tilting her head

      to that vine of hesitation   to be touched

as some men might

      brush their arms against each other

        without looking at themselves in the eye

           and in this way was the camera invented.

I Broke My Heart Said the Man in Rattan

I broke my heart, said the man in rattan,

      as he sang a song in clippings.

How special it was—that feeling—to be broken.

A clutter of *things*

      that could become the pretext for a painting

of Place. If only it held him: twig to needle, to groove.

A public loneliness made mainstay to the day itself

      so the inside become the outside

to be seen by the shape of a shell battered,

      and bent on a wall to become decoration.

How fortunate to be gathered,

      he thought, as if by accident.

There was a chair to sit on.

There was a shirt.

Fiesta

Fiesta of the older sister.

Fiesta of a boy.

Fiesta of the in-the-distance-against-the-sky-there-was-an-electric-tower.

Fiesta of a wire-mesh pattern.

There was a crowd, once, I imagined I could be gathered around.

Fiesta of the boy with a sombrero looking first at the float, then at the crowd,

then scrambling for the mise en scène, forging a skirt out of town he could be

left in if he did not cling to the rung.

Fiesta of the shoulder to shoulder I could faint.

Fiesta of the shadow of a suit that on this day will be sackcloth, in the husk, in the rind.

Fiesta of the loss of consciousness.

Fiesta of the waking up to find a stranger pressing his thumb and a world as a rope of

embarrassment hand in hand.

I held his hand, I told him. Again and again.

Bodas de Plata de Ñico. José M. Cuesta
Personajes que tomaron parte en el
Cuadro Poblo teatral, por
Don Venancio Barrcamo

The Mountain Fell

The mountain fell but there was no mountain
The sword found its way to the heart

      But even if the trembling lip of the actor

      Was any indication that the tip had hit the mark

Of the curl of yesteryear, that beautiful page,
Faithful even now to the script of his brow—

      In the arms of a lover—At the foot of a brother—

      In the ruffle of a sleeve meant to disconcert the world

into believing that the angle made by the neck against the lap

      of a neighbor was an indicator that the worst was over.

A flock of sheep moved in the distance.

           A door opened to a cliff which was really the curtain parted

      for that *one more time* which was really a feeling prolonged in the dark.

There was no gash in the head and yet there it flowed.

Like That Metaphor Heard Before

The nature of a city depends on the possibility that the woman on the cover of a magazine was the sister of a sister of your mother's friend.

I heard her name once, then I forgot. She was my sister, then my brother, then she was not.

The nature of a city depends on the possibility that there was a sea one could run to on the weekends. Legs laid bare, shirtless. The hair slick, shorts. The way my mother looked and looked into the distance as a way of thinking while being watched by my father. Then he stopped.

A picture is a happy place of somewhere far enough to think it will be better when you're there.

The sea was the green of yestermorn, the *S* of a title, a discount price tag folded, torn. The sand was the brown of not so nice. It could have been better. The arm would wither. The hair would fall. The shoe would lose its sparkle in the water. The smile would turn into that blurry picture of looking at nowhere in particular. It was a joke that was kept in my father's wallet that made him laugh.

The trouble with a photograph is that there is always a somewhere-else story.

There was a famous warrior with a rose—and who could forget that.

The Nature of a City

The nature of a city depends on the combination of views it could be seen from: by high noon or night, by backstreet or avenue. The electric poles were taller than the trees, at least in the photograph. And in the distance between the fire station and that huddle of makeshift dwellings that the multitudes constituted to form the soft machinery of the city, there were different implications on the detritus of corrugated steel and rubber. Plywood against the shadow-frame of a tributary of flowers! Carpet the shape of the foot of the chair that pressed onto it. A little statue of a cat. A drink coaster that soaked the moisture from a glass. The way a body floating for days could, by the density of the sea, decompose a face faster than one could say: "at the particular turn of that road," "we could simultanously see backrest, mountain, shore."

I Could Say

As when a boy folds the sleeves of his shirt up
to that spot on his elbow where there is enough
of his arm to say: *well.*

Or when a man lifts his daughter
and shakes her while in his mind he holds another.

By the tightness of a tie, the looseness of a stance,
a man is measured. If you can't walk straight, dear sir,
at least sit straight.

There was a smile to be made
with one's mouth closed and the full force of joy
that depended for its documentation
on that double-tandem armament of cheek and eye.

A chandelier shook, but whether this
was any indicator that the house was alright
and there was no need to regard the neighbor
from afar was as much the son's guess as anyone's.

The sheen of the picture
was always in the holder
dear History of mine.

There Are Fourteen Ways

There are fourteen ways to say *I might.*

Fifty ways to turn the tide.

Two kitchens: one dry.

There is a picture of a room within a room

within a brightly lit afternoon where my aunt sat

staring at the bougainvillea until the day it died.

She fell to the ground three times but then stood up,

while the men in the kitchen sat after the meal had been set

eyeing the silver she had gathered

the lacquer: thirteen, fourteen.

She began each morning with hot water.

She lived on a diet of fish.

There was a chair but she didn't sit on *that.*

She was my aunt.

The Nature of a City

The nature of a city is that it is built for someone else. Otherwise, a covenant.
Otherwise, a show. A script was written for the hero but only on the premise that
after a long bout of a lovebird illness, she was willing to be someone else. Four men
did not equal four men unless the last one standing was laughing. As on a church
ceiling, five devils flicked their tails snickering against the sun while a god sat on
his throne and by the gesture of his right hand extolled the virtues of humanity's
diminishment. Outside, the bazaars gave and gave, but there was not enough space
for: hemp, rope, basket, stone, fruit, market, screw, driver, cabinet, glow. There were
toys peddled outside in the street where you pulled and pulled that monkey of the
self and it climbed without reaching anywhere other than itself.

As If Water Had Been Made Out of

As if water had been made out of
the thin spout from which it came.
Or the gurgle of a gurgle. Or a stream.

You can take a man out of town,
but you can't make the rain not become
that downpour downslope route

every river knows it is headed for.
I went on a trip once,
but then it erased my face.

All I could remember was the pretty
painting of a vase that reminded me
of the flower dear postponement could be.

It could be a window. Or a tree.

Now That the Heart Has Stopped

Now that the heart has stopped.

Now that the hair is kept snug by a pin sharpened against jaw dust

And the pañuelito and the kamiseta have been fused into that long brocade of gauze

Spectatorship against the sweat of the nape : no : joe : no : collar : no : hold : now: that

There are separate pieces to touch.

The pattern was set on wood.

A fan rested on a chair unfurled

While the arm twitched behind some screen meant to ward off the fly, flick

The teeth a sight to behold, dear

Master. If only the lips be parted

While someone played that record score of coral salt

And physics: the painting of my grandmother:

The death of décor : that complicated mantelpiece of my home.

Standstill, Stasis

The way the river carried a boat.

*

The way a boy and his shimmer stood
at the edge of the stream unthinking.

*

Before the invention of the telephone.
Before the construction of the tram

*

that would take the flowers down from that mossy
mountaintop to that sweltering town.

*

It takes a man willing to walk up and down a village
to determine how long it would take the aster to wilt

*

in the neighbor's garden, inside a vase. There is a fruit
plucked without asking, like a letter stuffed

*

with one's thoughts fresh as the underbelly
of not saying. Unbruised.

*

Unpromised. After the war was lost.
After the refrigerator, upon invention, was defrosted.

The History of Towns

The history of towns is always
the history of looking back

Where is the belltower?
There is a tree and it still stands.

A family is only as good as the father
who is gone. A brother

with a son. A daughter who is only
as good as a vase of roses

which meant *very* good.

I never lived to see—
which did not mean that I had died

before the city had a train
that would have allowed me

to cross the length of an island
and stare at the sea

but there, there I stood.

Farewell Goodbye but Not Really

Or a nod done out of instinct
Or a sir in the room still sleeping
with his legs open this far into the morning
when every other dear gentleman
would be walking in the light.

There was a ship and it was sailing.
There was a group of men standing in line
looking in the same direction, suggesting that a war
was happening but only somewhere far

beyond the sheen of a photograph of a sea
seen on the edge of a hat, or the prow of a boat,
which was really the sheen of me trying hard
to be a boy, arm against my hip so only
a splinter could tremble my lip.

I would like to thank the designer of my dress
for the ribbon around my chest
so in the event of any future misdemeanor,
I will have the luxury of an apology
with a flower on my heart.

Farewell, goodbye,
but not really.
Imagine that you are out on a stroll merely

as in a game of kings and queens

where you closed the flower

(Walk.)

and you opened the flower

(Walk.)

and then you turned around.

Now There Is Only a Station

Now there is only a station and the sky.

A man stands on the side of the tracks.

Four potted plants. A lamp.

The theory of time is always a theory of sentimentality.

(1) He is waiting in vain for a train that will never arrive.

(2) He has been left behind.

(3) He arrived early.

For every theory, there is a simpler story, more funny.

A man sits in a corner, covers his face with his hands,

and breaks down in laughter.

Two birds alight on two trees, one covered in flowers,

the other barren, each one tempting the other

into or out of the leaves.

A wreck is a souvenir of a long time waiting.

A Parade Was a Way of Walking

A parade was a way of walking around town—   but with music.

Hear the brass band play, the accordion.   Or to look at houses

with their windows open.   The way a parasol   is first opened and

then

held against the sun.   The fan unfurled

so from now on the shielded face   would not be mistaken

for that passerby.   A parade was a way of finding someone

without looking   now that the only direction was forward.

And then around.   Is that a father

or his beautiful son?   The bald one.

The one who wore a hat.

There was a man with a round face who looked like he was about to smile.

There was a woman looking down.

Sometimes it was enough of a relief   to know that that year,

the tallest tree was still left standing   and the inability to make do

with what one had just been given—   the smell of flowers, a glance—

was still part of a century-old plan

that one without any evident reason still believed in.

A parade is a way of walking around a town without leaving.

CREDITS

The photographs in this book were taken from the archives of the Cebuano Studies Center (University of San Carlos), which contains the best collection of early-twentieth-century photographs in Cebu. These photographs cover the early part of the US occupation of the Philippines (1900–1946). Many of them are donations from private family collections. Unfortunately, the photographers are not mentioned in the records. My immense gratitude to the center for granting me permission to use the photographs in this book.

ACKNOWLEDGMENTS

This book would not have been possible without the generosity and support of family, friends, and teachers.

To Jee and Kim, and the rest of Gaudy Boy, for being the patient caretakers of this book.

To the editors at the Asian American Writers' Workshop where "The Experiment of the Tropics" first appeared (October 31, 2017). This poem subsequently received an honorable mention at the inaugural 2018 Hawker Prize for Southeast Asian Poetry. Thanks to the judges!

To the Nonfiction Writing Program of The University of Iowa, where I began writing this book and whose company provided the best kind of stimulation any writer could ask for. To the Fox Head and to Ronalds St. and to the long winters and all the friendships made during that time, which continue to sustain me now, many years after. A special shout-out to the Stanley Grant for allowing that quick trip back to the Philippines one summer, resulting in the initial encounter with these photographs.

To Washington University in St. Louis, especially Mary Jo Bang, whose mentorship provided the necessary space to understand what it meant for a writer to write away from his home and to begin to bend his language in ways that were both dangerous and exciting. A huge thank you to the Fulbright Scholarship for making this wonderful time in the Midwest possible.

To my teachers at the Ateneo de Manila University who encouraged me to look to history, if not for answers, then for questions.

To the Yale-NUS community, especially the students whose writing continues to challenge and extend my own love for poetry.

To the Wrice Residency of RMIT for providing the opportunity to share earlier drafts of this work with writers from the region.

To the artists and writers in Cebu and other parts of Southeast Asia who keep me grounded and whose work inspires me to continue the difficult task of writing about home in spite of difficult times.

And to all the friends I have made in the different cities I have found myself in. Your warmth and care have made this vagrant's life a little less lonely and have sustained me through all the years of wandering. Thank you for allowing me to ask the difficult questions you know I like to ask. Thank you for staying up longer than one should, and for laughing harder than necessary.

And, of course, to my family: Dad, Mom, Broddy, Hazel, and Arie. Thank you for all the stories of the old town and for the rich heritage of home. Thank you for giving me the freedom to pursue a life of writing. Thank you for the love, without which this writing would mean nothing.

ABOUT THE AUTHOR

Lawrence Lacambra Ypil is a poet and essayist from Cebu, Philippines. He has received an MFA in Nonfiction Writing from the University of Iowa and an MFA in Poetry from Washington University in St Louis on a Fulbright Scholarship. His first book of poems, *The Highest Hiding Place* (2009), was given the Madrigal-Gonzalez Best First Book Award. His work has received numerous awards, including The Academy of American Poets Prize, the Philippines Free Press Awards, and the Don Carlos Palanca Memorial Awards. His work explores the intersection of text and image, poetry and prose, and the role of material culture in the construction of cultural memory and identity. He teaches creative writing at Yale-NUS College in Singapore.

© Jona Branzuela Bering

ABOUT GAUDY BOY

From the Latin *gaudium,* meaning "joy," Gaudy Boy is a new literary press publishing Asian writing from Asia and America that seeks to delight readers.

The name is taken from the poem "Gaudy Turnout" by Singaporean poet Arthur Yap about his time abroad in Leeds, UK. Similarly inspired, Gaudy Boy seeks to bring literary works by authors of Asian heritage to the attention of an American audience.

We publish poetry, fiction, and creative non-fiction. To submit a manuscript, please query Jee Leong Koh at jkoh@singaporeunbound.org with a book proposal.

Established in 2018, Gaudy Boy is an imprint of the literary nonprofit Singapore Unbound. Visit our website at www.singaporeunbound.org/gaudyboy.

Other Gaudy Boy titles include:

Autobiography of Horse by Jenifer Sang Eun Park
Malay Sketches by Alfian Sa'at

CPSIA information can be obtained
at www.ICGtesting.com
Printed in the USA
LVHW082308090419
613597LV00003B/38/P

9 780982 814253